BARNABY CONRAD ESSAY   MARC MUENCH PHOTOGRAPHY

SANTA BARBARA

Photographs © MMIV by Marc Muench
Essay © MMIV by Barnaby Conrad
Photos: pages 21, 47, 49, 50, 56, 57, 61, 81, 83-88, 98, 105 © MMIV
by Bonnie Muench; page 81 © MMIV by Zandria Muench; pages
51, 59 © MMIV by Tom Dietrich; page 23 © by Roger Millikan

Library of Congress Cataloging-in-Publication Data

Muench, Marc.
  Santa Barbara / photography by Marc Muench ; essay by
Barnaby Conrad. ·
     p. cm.
  ISBN 1-55868-742-4 (hardbound)
  1. Santa Barbara (Calif.)—Pictorial works. 2. Santa Barbara
(Calif.)—Description and travel. I. Conrad, Barnaby, 1922– II. Title.
  F869.S45M845 2004
  979.4'91—dc22   2004005996

Graphic Arts Books
An imprint of Graphic Arts Center Publishing Company
P.O. Box 10306, Portland, Oregon 97296-0306
503-226-2402; www.gacpc.com

President: Charles M. Hopkins
Associate Publisher: Douglas A. Pfeiffer
Editorial Staff: Timothy W. Frew, Tricia Brown, Jean Andrews,
  Kathy Howard, Jean Bond-Slaughter
Production Staff: Richard L. Owsiany, Heather Doornink
Designer: Bonnie Muench
Digital Pre-press: Tom Dietrich

Printed in the United States of America

◀◀◀ The Santa Barbara Courthouse, built in 1929
◀◀ The City of Santa Barbara, nestled in between the Pacific
Ocean and the Santa Ynez Mountains
▶ The Santa Barbara Mission Bell Towers
▶▶ Pelicans in flight over Stearns Wharf

▲ Santa Barbara County Courthouse

▶ City view from the Courthouse clock tower

▼ Local fishing fleet moored in the Santa Barbara Harbor

▼ Afternoon stroll along Leadbetter Beach

▶ El Presidio de Santa Barbara State Historic Park, established in 1782

▼ El Presidio de Santa Barbara Chapel, the first church for the townspeople

▼ Snow-covered chaparral at 3,000 feet in the Santa Ynez Mountains

▶▶ The Santa Barbara Mission, founded in 1786 by Father Junípero Serra

▼ View of the Channel Islands from the Douglas Family Preserve above Hendry's Beach

▶ Outdoor dining at Paseo Nuevo

▼ Paseo Nuevo Shopping Mall, downtown Santa Barbara

▶ The historic Granada

Theatre on State Street,

the oldest standing movie

palace in the city

Spanish tiles on the Mission roof, the architectural style for the city of Santa Barbara.

▲ I Madonnari chalk art festival in May at the Mission

◀ Chalk paintings benefit the Children's Creative Project

▲ Snowy plovers

◀ Coal Oil Point, the beginning of the Gaviota Coast

◀ Elephant Seal Cove, Santa Barbara Island, Channel Islands National Park

▲ Garibaldi fish in the kelp forest off Santa Barbara Island

▶▶Sunrise over the east end of Anacapa Island, Channel Islands National Park

◀ Wild mustard near

Mission Canyon

▶ Lupine and the California

poppy on the slopes of

Figueroa Mountain

▲ Surfer in the morning hours at Campus Point

▶ Glen Annie Golf Course overlooking the Goleta Valley and Santa Cruz Island

▲ The Santa Barbara Harbor

▶ Adobe oven at the historic El Presidio

▲ Bougainvillea near the Arlington Theater

▶▶ La Cumbre Peak, rising 3,995 feet above Santa Barbara

▼ Sailboats in the Santa Barbara Channel

▼ Hang glider over the Pacific after launching from the Santa Ynez Mountains

▲ Along Foxen Canyon Wine Trail

▶ Koehler Vineyards in the Santa Ynez Valley

▼ Late afternoon at Stearns Wharf

▶▶ Stearns Wharf, completed in 1872, making it the longest deepwater pier between Los Angeles and San Francisco

▼ Rollerbladers and pedalinas along East Beach bike path

▼ Sunrise over Stearns Wharf

◀ Seagulls

▼ Sport diver filling his bag with a calico bass

▼ Santa Barbara County Courthouse tiles

W. A. Auden once remarked that no two people ever read the same book; in a like manner no two people ever choose the same reasons to live in Santa Barbara. Generally acknowledged to be one of America's most beautiful and charming cities, it was a good deal less than that when João Rodrigues Cabrilho, more commonly known as Juan Cabrillo, first landed at what was then a Chumash village, on October 13, 1542. The Portuguese explorer, in the service of Spain, first anchored off of what is now known as the Rincon, a favorite spot for serious surfers.

A creek runs into the ocean there, and the men came ashore to fill their barrels with fresh water. Cabrillo was uncommonly pleased with the Chumash Indian village: "Fine canoes each holding twelve or thirteen Indians came to the ships," he wrote. "They have round houses, well covered down to the ground."

As so many modern visitors do today, Cabrillo decided to spend the winter in these splendid environs. Who knows how much longer he would have stayed, but, alas, he died a few months later after a fall on San Miguel Island.

My own Santa Barbara adventure began with a bang—a huge, devastating, historical bang. It was June 29, 1925, and I had arrived with my nine-year-old brother and our German governess on the Lark, the night sleeper from San Francisco to Los Angeles. Since the train stopped so early in the morning at Santa Barbara, that special car was regularly shunted off to a siding where passengers slept or waited until a decent hour to be picked up. Our father was to pick us up at seven and take us to our grandmother's home for a week's holiday.

At 6:23 the city's most devastating earthquake struck, rocking the Pullman car back and forth on its rails, and terrifying my brother, our governess, and me. I was only three years old, but I remember vividly my nurse screaming—the first time I had ever seen a grown-up cry.

The initial quake was centered on an offshore fault, but it was the two aftershocks, five minutes apart, that did the greatest damage. Most downtown buildings were destroyed. The front of the big Arlington Hotel fell off, and it was said that it resembled an open dollhouse, with most of the rooms still intact. However, a 60,000-gallon water tank toppled from its tower and plowed through the ceiling of some luxury suites, killing two people.

Remarkably, only twelve people were killed on that terrible day, but the town was destroyed. Even the city's beloved and beautiful mission, built in 1786, was badly damaged. (The original mission building had already been destroyed in Santa Barbara's first severe earthquake in 1812.)

Ironically, this destructive quake was directly responsible for much of Santa Barbara's present beauty. Before the quake, Santa Barbara was a pretty ordinary-looking

◀ Bougainvillea

▼ Paseo Nuevo architecture

twentieth-century California town, devoid of the red tiles and Spanish architecture that give it such character today. Santa Barbara has always boasted a spectacular location, of course, with the majestic mountains behind the vast beaches, but the architecture itself was nothing to write home about. Two local residents, Bernard Hoffman and Pearl Chase, led a campaign for Santa Barbara to capitalize on its Spanish origins and return to that long-ago look. After the quake, under the powerful Architectural Advisory Committee, Spanish-style buildings began to dot the devastated downtown, historical buildings were restored, and a unique city was created. Pearl Chase was such a dominant and influential citizen and so dedicated to keeping the town Spanish that she convinced the Southern Pacific Railroad to build their roundhouse on East Beach to resemble a bullring in Spain. When the Standard Oil Company wanted to install a gas station where the huge Moreton Bay Fig holds court, she mounted a campaign to save the majestic tree, and it still stands there today near the train station.

The Moreton Bay Fig was planted by a little girl in 1876, after she received a seedling from a sailor recently returned from Moreton Bay, Australia. Though called a fig tree, it is actually a *Ficus macrophylla*, a cousin of the rubber tree, and it is believed to be the largest of its species in the world.

So the earthquake was my introduction to the marvelous state of mind, some ninety miles north of Los Angeles, called Santa Barbara; I would eventually end up spending the last half of my life here. Though I was born and brought up in San Francisco, my family visited Santa Barbara often, staying either with my grandmother or at the venerable (and then ultra chic) Miramar Hotel on the beach. My wife and I moved here in 1970 and, like so many others who have settled in this remarkable town, we are here to stay.

SANTA BARBARA: A GUIDED TOUR. I love to show visiting friends around Santa Barbara—showing them the sites, the attractions, the out-of-the-way places, and, in doing so, teaching a little bit of the history of this wonderful place.

The first thing most people comment on is the plethora of all things Spanish, starting with the names of the streets: Indio Muerto, Quarantina, Cañon Perdido (Lost Cannon), and Salsipuedes (get out if you can). When the Catholic hospital was built at Micheltorena and Salsipuedes Streets, it was originally named "Salsipuedes Hospital," much to the amusement of the Spanish-speaking residents. It was hastily changed to "St. Francis Hospital."

As for the naming of Cañon Perdido, or "Lost Cannon

Street," in the winter of 1847, just after the United States had taken possession of California, the brig *Elizabeth* ship-wrecked on East

◀ Summerland Beach

▼ Surfers at Arroyo Burro Beach

Beach, and one of its cannons went missing. Afraid that pro-Mexican factions had stolen it to attack American troops, Col. R. B. Mason, the military governor of California, declared that Santa Barbara citizens be fined $500 for the missing weapon. The citizens thought this ridiculous, refused to pay, and when the missing cannon was found buried in the sand ten years later, they paraded it through town, named a street after it, and put a picture of it on Santa Barbara's first seal.

Santa Barbara's history and people are captured in the names of its streets: Ortega, De la Guerra, Carrillo, Gutierrez, Cota for the city founders and prominent citizens. Victoria, Micheltorena, Sola, Figueroa for the Mexican governors, Mason for an American governor, and Anapamu and Yanonali for the most important Chumash chieftains.

First, I drive visitors to the County Courthouse on Anacapa Street and watch their jaws drop when they take in the lines of the elegant eighty-five-foot clock tower and the great arch below it, and the bravura murals inside. Considered by many to be the most beautiful government building in America, the Courthouse, lawn, and gardens occupy an entire square block.

We continue on to Mission Street, round a corner, and there looms the Santa Barbara Mission, its twin towers restored to pink perfection after the quake.

The Old Mission, as it's affectionately known, is the icon of Santa Barbara. More than two centuries old and the tenth of California's twenty-one missions, the then tule-thatched shelter of logs was dedicated by Friar Fermín

Lasuen on December 4, 1786. From the time it was first built, the Mission was a center of the town's activities, and the King of Spain sent two bells to call the faithful to worship. The beautiful structure was finally completed in 1820; it is the only mission in the state to have been occupied uninterruptedly by the Franciscan Order. It is continually busy with both secular and non-secular events and tens of thousands of tourists visit its museum, gift shop, and, especially in the spring, its beautiful rose garden. Every Memorial Day weekend, the plaza of the Old Mission is transformed into a color-splashed canvas during the I Madonnari Italian Street Painting Festival. Skilled sidewalk artists decorate the pavement with intricate reproductions of famous paintings, with the proceeds from the event going to help maintain the Mission.

After a tour of the Mission, I usually take visitors around the corner to the Botanic Garden on Mission Canyon Road. Its sixty-five acres of trails offer rare plants, incredible sweeping views of the Channel Islands, redwoods, and an ancient aqueduct used by the Franciscan padres in the old days.

And if they are not too exhausted, the Museum of Natural History is right there on Puesta de Sol Road. The museum features eleven exhibit halls that focus on regional natural history, including birds, insects, mammals, marine life,

paleontology, Native Americans, and the Chumash Indians. The Lizard Lounge features live reptiles and amphibians.

And if they are not gardened out, a quick stop at the Alice Keck Park Memorial Garden is right downtown, two blocks west of State Street. Dedicated in 1980, the park features streams and ponds of huge koi plus gazebos, bridges, and footpaths.

The next stop on my tour is lunch in the old Paseo or the Paseo Nuevo; two areas in downtown Santa Barbara, which, though modern, physically duplicate the look of the long-ago Spanish and Mexican rule. Here one finds restaurants, sidewalk cafés, antique shops, boutiques, and art galleries.

After lunch: The Santa Barbara Museum of Art on the city's main seven-mile thoroughfare, State Street. An imposing building for such a small town, its entranceway displays a magnificent collection of Greek and Roman statues donated years ago by philanthropist Wright Ludington, and there is always an interesting temporary exhibition in the main gallery.

A couple of blocks away is the oldest continual theater in the west, the stately Lobero. Santa Barbara has long been a town of pageants and parades and theater, going back to the early Spanish days. But the man who created California's first community theater was not Spanish or Mexican but came to Santa Barbara from Italy. He called himself José Lobero and he started a saloon with an orchestra at State and Cañon Perdido Streets. This soon led to grand opera with José designing the sets, training

amateurs for the parts, managing the orchestra, singing the leading roles, and, incidentally, running a successful saloon. Eventually the productions outgrew the saloon, and Lobero built a proper theater using an old adobe for its foyer and balcony. Opening in 1872, the new theater presented its first performance, an opera directed by, written by, produced by, and starring, who else? José Lobero.

The Lobero soon became the social and cultural hub of the city, but somehow José lost his money and disappeared. The theater managed to survive, and, in 1924, a new and lovely Lobero Theater was built. The grand opening fiesta for the new Lobero became the inspiration for the Old Spanish Days Fiesta celebrated to this day for one wild week every August. The Lobero is still the focal point of Santa Barbara's lively theatrical attractions.

An even grander theater opened on April 9, 1924, on State Street, with a silent film, *Mademoiselle Midnight*. The elegant Granada Theatre not only showed films but also presented musicals, plays, and symphonies. It was a favorite place for Hollywood previews and premieres. Ask anyone where *Gone with the Wind* was first shown; they'll probably say Atlanta. Nope—it was the Granada. The theater still operates, and it is one of the main sites of the Santa Barbara International Film Festival.

Now I steer visitors down to the harbor, past the welcoming fountain of huge leaping porpoises, sculptor Bud Bottoms's work, and out onto Stearns Wharf. Here there are fish markets, shops, a maritime museum, and a few seafood restaurants. (For superior seafood we'd go a mile north to the yacht harbor to Santa Barbara's favorite, the unpretentious but delicious Brophy's, which overlooks the nearly 1,200 boats in the harbor.) The original breakwater, a 900-foot promontory, was completed in 1929, the result of the financial clout of yeast mogul Max Fleischmann, who later contributed a quarter of a million dollars to extend it 600 feet to accommodate safe anchorage for his 250-foot yacht.

Coming out of the yacht harbor we hang a right and head down Cabrillo Street past the myriad volleyball players and sun worshippers on the wide and beautiful beach, past actor Fess Parker's sprawling DoubleTree Resort, and we come to Niños Drive and the Santa Barbara Zoological Gardens. We just have to stop, especially if there are children with us.

The zoo is a delight. With thirty acres of lush gardens spread across a knoll overlooking the Pacific Ocean, it has more than seven hundred animals including three Western lowlands gorillas, elephants, giraffes, and lions, plus a little train and a carousel for kids.

This zoo was opened to the public in 1963, but prior to that the only zoo in the Santa Barbara area was in Montecito. A zoo in Montecito? Most people aren't aware that there once was a real zoo in the heart of that elegant enclave, right off East Valley Road. Christian Holmes, of the Fleischmann yeast family, an eminent physician originally from Cincinnati, Ohio, came to Santa Barbara in the 1920s and built a great estate in Montecito, which he called Featherhill Ranch. He started collecting exotic birds, and then branched off into wild animals after providing a retirement cage for the original and aging Leo the Lion, the roaring trademark of Metro-Goldwyn-Mayer. There followed other animals, and by the end of 1924 there were bears, mountain lions, a tiger, and an elephant. One night in 1932, Holmes's wife, actress Katherine McDonald of the silent screen, had a terrifyingly real nightmare; the tiger had gotten loose and killed her young son. Subsequently the animals were all sent to San Francisco to form the nucleus of the Fleishhacker Zoo, and the estate was sold.

My first encounter with the present-day zoo occurred before I even moved to Santa Barbara. I had owned a very popular nightspot in San Francisco for ten years where celebrities celebrated. When I finally decided to sell it in 1962, I wanted to find a nice retirement spot for four huge parrots who had held vigil in the nightclub behind a glass enclosure. I wrote to the Santa Barbara

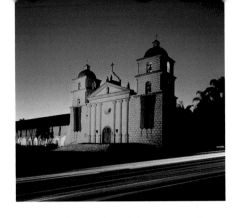

◀ Dusk at the Santa Barbara Mission

▼ Santa Barbara Roasting Company in Paseo Nuevo

Zoo asking if they would like four splendid macaws for free. I had an immediate answer by telegram.

"We accept your generous offer, of course, and await the birds' arrival eagerly. Please inform immediately their previous habitat so that we might duplicate exactly."

I was tempted to answer: "Put the birds in a soft-lit smoky room and keep them up until 2:00 A.M. every night with a background of alcohol-slurred voices, a thumping bass, and a stride piano. Let them hear lots of boozy small talk sprinkled with some genuine esoteric conversation, quite a few dialogues of seduction, marital discords, happy celebrations, the many varied vagaries of the human condition, and so forth. Helpful if you could get such recent admirers as Rita Hayworth, John Steinbeck, and Frank Sinatra to visit occasionally."

But instead I wired: "Bringing birds down to you Monday and will explain their previous environment. If I can."

My most recent connection with the zoo occurred four years ago after the death of an elderly actress, Laura Varden, who had played minor roles such as the house-keeper in *The Sound of Music* among other things. Several years earlier, she had brought her sick cat, Daisy, into the zoo officials, and they saved her beloved pet. In gratitude she promised to leave the zoo "a little something" in her will. The little something turned out to be close to a million dollars. With the money the zoo redesigned the reception area to the facility, and in memory of the benefactor they commissioned me to sculpt a bronze portrait of a

sleeping Daisy on a boulder, which today greets visitors when they enter.

Upon leaving the zoo on my guided tour, the road takes us past the little lake of the Andre Clark Bird Refuge and then past the green hills of the Cemetery, which, with its spectacular view of the Pacific Ocean, has been called the most beautiful in America. "Beautiful" juxtaposed with "Cemetery" might seem the ultimate oxymoron, but in this case it is true.

If we stay on the road that runs along the ocean, we soon come to the famous old Biltmore, now a Four Seasons operation. An elegant and expensive hotel, it also boasts the glamorous Coral Casino across the road, which features individual cabanas, restaurants, and an Olympic-sized swimming pool.

As long as we are in Montecito we should visit Lotusland. This is the estate of Madame Ganna Walska, whose gardens are world famous. She was a Polish beauty and opera singer whose main talent was marrying rich men—six of them—including a Russian baron and Harold McCormick of the International Harvester Company. Her

passion lay in gardens, and her amazing estate is covered with plants from all over the world, plus ponds and a terraced outdoor

54

◀ Historic Stow House in Goleta

▼ Old Town Trolley and the Courthouse

theater decorated with stone figures brought from her French chateau. She died in 1984, close to one hundred years old, but today a foundation maintains the gardens in pristine form, and the estate is open to visitors by advance arrangement.

A couple of miles below Lotusland, on the left-hand side of the highway, is the tiny town of Summerland, made up of wall-to-wall antique shops and restaurants.

Continuing down Highway 101 we pass the city's celebrated polo fields, where there always seems to be a game going on. The Sport of Kings has been popular in Santa Barbara since the twenties. I like to remind people that when I was a boy three of the top players were Wack, Wallop, and Gallup—and it is true!

On the right of the highway past the polo fields we pass the little town of Santa Claus—and yes, Virginia, there is a town of that name, or more properly, a street of stores and two restaurants that calls itself a town; a long-standing giant figure of Santa Claus was, mercifully, removed in 2003.

A few miles further is a real town, called Carpinteria. The name means "carpenter shop," and this is where, in ancient days, the Chumash Indians would build and repair the great canoes that they used for fishing and even whaling. It is an old-fashioned, attractive California town that has changed little over the years; I happen to know because the Cate School is located high on a mesa over-looking the town and the orange and avocado orchards, and I attended the school when I was fourteen and fifteen years old. To me the main change in the looks of

the town is that there are no hitching rails in front of the hamburger spots. In my day, all seventy of the Cate boys were required to have horses, and the merchants of Carpinteria were eager for our business. The founder and headmaster, Curtis W. Cate, felt that caring for a horse built character in his students, and we did enjoy the horse activities, the roping contests, the dressage, and the gymkhana competition with other horsy schools.

Back then, it was a different world, a very different world. Today, along with the hitching posts, Ober's Hamburger Emporium has been replaced by The Spot, and almost as much Spanish is heard spoken around town as when Juan Rodríguez Cabrillo discovered Carpinteria and Santa Barbara.

Our brief overlook of Santa Barbara is ended.

But, one exclaims, what about the Danish-styled town of Solvang thirty minutes north of Santa Barbara? That quaint settlement with its giant windmill and myriad shops and restaurants and the nearby elegant ranch resort, Alisal, would require a book, or certainly a booklet, of its own.

And what about the wineries? Wineries and wine tasting have become very big in Santa Barbara in recent years. Probably the most visited wineries are Firestone and Fess Parker. The former actor turned hotelier and vintner owns the charming little hotel and restaurant in Los Olivos called Fess Parker's Wine

▼ Morning fog at the Goleta Pier

Country Inn. The little town's many shops and galleries also offer the tasting of wine from about two dozen wines from nearby wineries.

Santa Barbara has always been a mecca for artists, and my most treasured moments from those days were the times when I would get a lift into Santa Barbara and have the great cowboy artist Ed Borein critique my crude attempts at painting. He had a studio in the old Paseo designed to look like a street in Spain. A bronze plaque there informs tourists where his studio was.

"Stop copying photos out of magazines," he would scold. "Draw and paint from life! Here—sit down and draw me that chair—see how the light streaming from the window catches the spokes of the backrest? If you can draw that chair, just the way it is with the pretty light hitting it just so, you'll be able to draw anything."

A classmate, Richard DeMille, introduced me to another artist, Joe DeYong, whose studio was only a block away from Borein's. Joe, who was stone-deaf and virtually mute, was also a fine cowboy artist, the protégé and adopted son of the famed Charles Russell of Montana. Joe had been hired by Richard's father, Cecil, to design the costumes for the epic film *The Plainsman*, starring Gary Cooper and Jean Arthur. Though Joe could only communicate by writing, he was a delightful guy. We became friends and he also gave me art instruction. (One can see fine examples of both Borein and DeYong's work in the Santa Barbara Historical Museum on De la Guerra Street.)

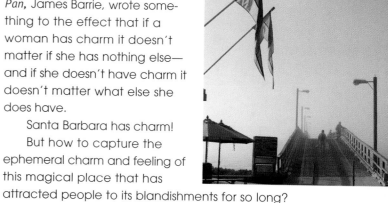

THE CHARM. The author of *Peter Pan*, James Barrie, wrote something to the effect that if a woman has charm it doesn't matter if she has nothing else—and if she doesn't have charm it doesn't matter what else she does have.

Santa Barbara has charm!

But how to capture the ephemeral charm and feeling of this magical place that has attracted people to its blandishments for so long?

Santa Barbara, because of its climate, beaches, and fine hotels, has been a resort town dating back to the 1860s. It also boasted several famous springs and spas (hence the prominent thoroughfares in Montecito: Hot Springs Road and Cold Springs Road). My great-grandmother, Mrs. Jerothumul Bowers Barnaby, was the first of my family to visit here. A wealthy widow from Rhode Island, she came to Santa Barbara in 1891 "for the waters and the pure air," as so many people from the East did in those days.

"I just love Santa Barbara!" she wrote a friend. She stayed at the very elegant Montecito Hot Springs Hotel, a luxurious spa, first made famous to America by the writer Charles Nordhoff. Three types of mineral springs (sulfur, arsenic, and iron) were the big draw as well as the luxurious accommodations and elaborate cuisine. (It burned down

▼ Shoreline Park palms in the fog

in 1920.) Some of the springs remain but are not available to the general public. Many were cemented over because of neighbors' complaints about the sulfurous fumes.

Unfortunately, Granny never made it home from her stay in Santa Barbara. After staying several weeks, she left by train to visit friends in Colorado on her way back to her mansion in Providence. While in Denver a package mailed from Boston caught up with her, containing a bottle with a note reading "Happy New year, accept this fine old whiskey from your friend in the woods." She drank of it and died five days later; it was not whiskey—it was plain water plus sixty-six grams of arsenic. The deed was pinned on her doctor, handsome T. Thacher Graves, who was mentioned in her will. Sentenced to be hanged, Graves chose, instead, to end his own life by soaking the flypaper in his cell in water and drinking it. Thus, he, too, died of arsenic poisoning.

Santa Barbara has always been known as a writer's haven, going way back to one of Hemingway's boyhood heroes, Stewart Edward White and his outdoor novels, and Charles Nordhoff, who with James Norman Hall, wrote *Mutiny on the Bounty.* In the 1920s, the Nobel Prize-winner John Galsworthy wrote some of his epic *Forsyte Saga* at the San Ysidro Ranch in Montecito. The beloved *Saturday Evening Post* writer Guy Gilpatric (the *Mister Glencannon* series), and Don Quinn who wrote the old radio show *Fibber McGee and Molly,* and Vic Morrow who created *The Cisco Kid* all worked out of Santa Barbara in the forties and fifties.

The famous Sinclair Lewis rented a house on Anacapa Street for a few months in 1946–47. I was in town visiting my parents at the time, so I screwed up my courage and wrote him a fan letter. To my amazement he invited me to tea via a note from his chauffeur.

At sixty-two he was a startling sight. I recoiled from the skeletal head, the sunken haunted eyes, and the scarlet pocked face. Yet after a few moments in his brilliant and humorous presence one forgot about his looks. We talked for an hour; he asked to see the first seventy-five pages of my novel, and he invited me to join him for dinner at the Casa de Sevilla. The restaurant, called Pete's by most people after the owner, Pete Egus, looked unprepossessing on the outside, but until 2002 it was the town's most popular and chic watering hole. Softly lit and graced with antique bullfight posters from Spain, it was a mecca for celebrities, socialites, and Hollywood stars.

This night Mr. Lewis had also invited a young couple he had only recently met. They turned out to be the writers Margaret and Ken Millar. (They would soon be famous novelists, she for her mysteries under her own name and he as Ross Macdonald.)

After they'd said goodnight and left, Mr. Lewis remarked:

◀ Sea anemone in tide pool

▼ Arroyo Burro Beach sea grass at low tide

"How I envy them!"

"Their talent?" I asked.

"Their marriage," poignantly replied the twice-divorced author.

The next day he suggested "getting rid of 72 of the 75 pages" I had given him. But he said there was "promise in those last three pages" and to give him 75 more. After reading them he telephoned me to say that "now your story's moving," and he hired me as a secretary-companion-protégé, and I spent the next five months at Thorvale, his 750-acre estate in Williamstown, Massachusetts.

Nowadays a great many well-known writers call Santa Barbara home, such as Sue Grafton, Fannie Flagg, Pico Iyer, T. Coraghessan Boyle, J. F. Freedman, Alan Folsom, Dennis and Gayle Lynds, as well as numerous screenwriters and television writers. Santa Barbara becomes a focus for aspiring authors the last week in June when four hundred writers converge for the Santa Barbara Writers Conference. Sci-fi guru Ray Bradbury has given the opening night speech for all of its more-than-three decades.

Another momentous event occurs on the same Saturday of the Writers Conference: the madly decadent Summer Solstice celebration. This is simply a one-day parade of many bizarre floats and costumes, some beautiful, some freakish, which results in sort of the New Orleans Mardi Gras meets the Rio Carnival on Downtown State Street.

A more sober and family-oriented affair is the venerable weeklong Santa Barbara Fiesta held every August, which features parades of great horseflesh, carriages, Spanish and Mexican costumes, music and dancing, and lots of eating and drinking.

A truly unique Santa Barbara tradition is the Rancheros Visitadores. It evolved from the old tradition of ranchers riding to their neighbors' spreads to help with the branding, calving, and haying. Then in the nineteen thirties a small group of gentlemen ranchers got together with friends and celebrities for a weeklong party inspired by San Francisco's famed annual Bohemian Grove clambake in the redwoods, the difference being that the Rancheros are on horseback most of the day. Now numbering more than a thousand members, tycoons, politicians, artists, writers, musicians, and actors start out from the Santa Barbara Mission the first Saturday of May and ride off to their 7,000-acre ranch near Lake Cachuma, camping and reveling along the way.

Celebrities have always gravitated to Santa Barbara, and not solely because of its proximity to Hollywood. John F. Kennedy and Jackie honeymooned at Santa Barbara's oldest hotel, the cottage-dotted hills of the San

Ysidro Ranch in Montecito, as did Laurence Olivier and Vivien Leigh.

One of the original owners of the San Ysidro Ranch was the

◀ Santa Barbara County Library

▼ Fog rolling in over the Mesa

esteemed actor Sidney Poitier. With great glee he tells the story of how upon leaving a board meeting at the hotel one morning he saw an older woman struggling with a suitcase as she emerged from a taxi. "Let me help you with that, Madame," he said, and followed her up to her cottage; she tipped him fifty cents.

Many people don't realize how close Santa Barbara came to being Hollywood; our city briefly housed the biggest movie studio in the world. By 1911, there were thirteen movie companies in Santa Barbara using the mountains and the ocean to portray everything from the Alps to the South Seas; even the offshore Channel Islands were used. The Flying A Company owned the first indoor movie set (at State and Mission Streets) and may have originated the first animated cartoons. Many fine directors got their starts here, including Victor Fleming, who came to the studio as a mechanic and many years later would direct such films as *Gone with the Wind* and *The Wizard of Oz.*

Eight years and some twelve hundred films later, the studios in Santa Barbara began moving to the Los Angeles area, mainly because they needed the big city streets and buildings for their stories. But the stars had discovered Santa Barbara's charms, and they bought or built homes here. Early residents were suave Ronald Colman, Warner Oland (the original Charlie Chan), the gorgeous Eleanor Boardman, and director King Vidor. A later wave included Robert Mitchum, Richard Widmark, Burl Ives, Jeff Bridges, Judith Anderson, Karl Malden, Jane Russell, Kirk Douglas, Eva Marie Saint, and Lena Horne. Today, one

knows that such mega stars as Oprah Winfrey live here behind the walls of their mega mansions, but one doesn't see them. In 2001, Miss Winfrey bought Tara II, the splendid Bacon estate in Montecito, for a reported fifty million dollars; the forty-acre estate, built in 1934, comprises a 19,826-square-foot Georgian mansion, 3,014-square-foot guest house, a barn, tennis court, pool, an orchard, several ponds, and a lake. Understandably, she has a staff of eleven.

On the other hand, one sees famed comedian Jonathan Winters everywhere. He loves to leave his mansion and wander around town trying out new "stuff" on surprised and pleased strangers. Recently at his favorite restaurant, the little sandwich shop in the Montecito Pharmacy, I saw him sit down with an elderly and startled matron whom he'd never met. "Do not be afraid, m'dear," he said in a put-on grandfatherly quaver, "I will not attack you—Mister Pencil doesn't write anymore." She laughed, finally, when she realized who he was.

At one time Santa Barbara was generally perceived as a stodgy refuge for the elderly rich and was the butt of many jokes: viz, a place where old people go to visit their parents; a haven only for the newly wed and the nearly dead; the orthopedic shoe set's Woodstock, etc. Twenty years ago, I asked the seventy-year-old actor John Ireland why he chose to live in Montecito, and he replied, "Because they call me kid here."

▼ Santa Barbara Museum of Art

But Santa Barbara has changed. While losing little of its old-world color and elegance, it seems to have been discovered by the outside world and to have been infused with a new, younger spirit. Los Angeles and San Francisco remain the cities that Santa Barbarans go to when they need shots of culture, and Santa Barbara remains a town—not a city—but it is a town with history, flare, and an old-world charm unique in America.

While a great many retired and rich people live here, and polo playing is still big, hordes of young people play volleyball on East Beach every day, world-class surfers come for the Rincon's waves, teenagers flock to concerts in the bowl, hikers of all ages enjoy the hills behind the city, freshwater and saltwater fishing and whale watching have devoted aficionados, tourists gape at the Arlington Theater's *trompe l'oeil* interior, the art museum on State Street is packed, the symphony thrives, the young Santa Barbara International Film Festival grows in prestige every year, the Music Academy of the West attracts musicians from all over the country every summer (held partly at the Jefferson mansion and partly at the Cate School), and the many fine restaurants thrive around the calendar. Some of the favorite eateries are the Café del Sol on the estuary, Piatti's and Pan e Vino in Montecito, The Nugget in Summerland, and Mollie's Trattoria on Coast Village Road (Oprah's favorite).

Santa Barbara charmed José Francisco de Ortega and Father Junípero Serra back in 1782 when they arrived to establish the last presidio and the first Spanish settlement at the site. "Me encanta!" Ortega is said to have exclaimed.

And the city continues to enchant both residents and the many visitors from around the world—estimated at more than eight million annually—who also succumb to its myriad charms.

As I write this on the porch of my Rincon Point home, adjacent to Montecito, the weather in mid-February is an unseemly 72 degrees, the sun is shining brightly, and across a wide expanse of beach, I am watching a dozen surfers skimming down the face of an eight-foot viridian wave. Fifty yards beyond the surfers a pod of porpoises frolic and fifty yards over my head a paraglider hangs dreamily on a never-ending thermal.

If I narrow my eyes, stretch my imagination, and go back 462 years, I can see the two historic caravels, the *San Salvador* and the *Victoria*, lying out there beyond the surf line, and Juan Cabrillo rowing in to shore in a skiff and about to land on what is now my front lawn.

Earlier this morning my wife had suggested we take a trip to Europe, and I replied, as do the people of Paris:

"Why travel? We are here!"

▼ Parapenting over the Santa Ynez Mountains

▲ A walk in the surf at Butterfly Beach

▲ Waterfront tile

▶ Early morning at the Santa Barbara Harbor

▲ Los Padres National

Forest from Figueroa

Mountain lookout

◀ Climber on "T-Crack,"

Gibraltar Rock

◀ Pampas grass above Goleta Beach

▼ Trail along East Camino Cielo Road

▶▶ Mountain biker descending from Figueroa Mountain Road

▲ Sea lions playing near Anacapa Island

▶ Campus Point and Goleta Beach

▼ Pelicans over Santa Barbara Harbor

▼ Clearing storm over the Channel Islands

▲ Dancers performing their favorite fiery flamenco dances during Old Spanish Days

◀ Fiesta dancer performing in the Sunken Gardens

▼ Fiesta celebration, Las Noches De Ronda "Nights of Gaiety"

▼ Santa Barbara County's tallest waterfall, Nojoqui Falls

▶ Andree Clark Bird Refuge from the Santa Barbara Zoo

▼ A Western lowland gorilla at the Santa Barbara Zoo

▶ "Cats of Africa" exhibit and zoo train

▼ Summer Solstice Parade on State Street

◀ Solstice parade float

▲ Fire Department friends

▲ Sea stars, anemone, and

mussels in coastal tidal pools

◀ Santa Barbara coast from

Goleta Point

◀ Turtle sliding into the garden pond

▼ Thunderheads reflected in the pond at Alice Keck Park Memorial Gardens

◀ Gazebo overlooking Alice Keck Park

▼ Garden paths at Alice Keck Park Memorial Gardens

◀ King Neptune fountain at Ganna Walska Lotusland Garden

▼ Lotus in bloom at Ganna Walska Lotusland Garden

◀ Egret fishing tide pools

▼ Andree Clark Bird Refuge

▼ Morning mist shrouding St. Anthony's Seminary tower

◀ Gulf Fritillary butterfly

▶▶ Surfing one of many breaks along Point Conception

◀ Mission dam and restored

aqueduct at the Santa

Barbara Botanic Garden

▶ Redwood forest along

Mission Creek, in the

Botanic Garden

▼ Stained glass at the Santa Barbara Maritime Museum

◀ Kelp forest in Channel Islands National Park

▼ Opportunities for all types of sailors off of East Beach

▶ Snow-covered sandstone boulder along East Camino Cielo Road

▼ Shoreline Park bluffs

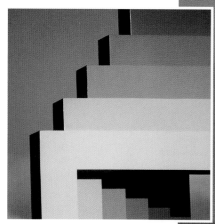

▲ Rainbow Arch along

Cabrillo Boulevard, named

Chromatic Gate by its

creator, Herbert Bayer

▶ The Santa Barbara Riviera

graced by a rainbow

▲ Poppies at the Goleta Train Depot

▶ Lake Los Carneros

◀ Imported handmade tiles

and wrought iron fixtures

adorning the Santa Barbara

County Courthouse

▶ The Mural Room, painted

by Dan Sayre Groesbeck

◀ *Spirit of the Ocean* fountain, Santa Barbara County Courthouse

▶▶ Bottlenose dolphins in the Santa Barbara Channel

◀ Commemorative tiles and

a golden trumpet tree at the

Courthouse

▶ Courthouse tiles

▼ State Street shops and La Arcada Plaza

▲ Entrance to the Santa Barbara Museum of Natural History

▼ Lighthouse on Anacapa Island, Channel Islands National Park

▼ Blue whale skeleton at the Museum of Natural History

◀ The University of California,

Santa Barbara (UCSB) Lagoon

▶ Sunset over Ellwood Mesa

▲ University of California, Santa Barbara (UCSB) Storke Plaza and Tower

▼ Valley fog below Zaca Peak, Los Padres National Forest

▲ Surfer at Rincon Point

◀ Santa Cruz Island at dawn

from Refugio State Park

◀ Wildflowers and oaks on Figueroa Mountain

▶▶ Biker descending Figueroa Mountain

Photographer's Notes

The images in this book reflect many diverse techniques, some incorporated for the first time. Whether noticeable or not, the methods used were a mixture of old and new. This is my first published book with digitally captured images. I don't believe it was a goal to be trendy, but rather, a discovery of a useful and/or superior outcome.

I have always tried to stay on the cutting edge of my profession and keep up with technological advancements, but during the three years of photographing this book, changes seemed to whiz by at a furious pace. I found myself using three different formats of film cameras, three new and completely different types of digital cameras, four different types of emulsions, including a new color negative from Kodak, and three different versions of Adobe Photoshop.

Since all the images are converted to digital for the reproduction of this and all modern-day books, I was able to maintain control over the color and style of the reproduction. This influenced the way I utilized both film and digital files. Many of the digitally captured images in this book are not easily recognizable. This was my intent to blend them in and only appreciate the advantages. Once film is scanned, it is incorporated into the very same workflow as a digitally captured image file. The tangible photograph becomes an intangible computer file during the editing process. It is then reborn as the final image when high resolution color proofs are made in our studio on an Epson printer. This is where I am able to make critical creative decisions about the contrast, color cast, and tone of an image. The digitally captured image files are not tangible until the final proofs are printed.

For the film images I used Kodak G and GX 100 speed transparency film as well as Kodak UC negative film on a few shots. I worked with a Canon 35mm EOS1v film camera and a Contax 6 x 4.5 film camera. For the digitally captured images I used two types of Canon cameras: the 10D and the 1Ds. I also used a Kodak DCS proback on my Contax medium format camera and a Kodak 14n camera. My favorite is now the Kodak DCS proback, which allows me to change between film and digital by using different backs on the same camera. For the large format images I used a Zone 6, 4x5 field camera with three lenses, Rodenstock 75mm grandegon, Fuginon 450mm telephoto, and an Osaka 210mm.

I used the different formats of cameras to capture unique types of images. My large 4x5 format works best for many landscapes and architectural images, while the small and medium formats, both film and digital, were useful for the more journalistic images with moving subjects, allowing me to respond to more spontaneous circumstances. I enjoyed the instant response from the digital cameras' LCD screen on the backs of the cameras. These allowed me to critique composition on the fly, and many times I corrected viewpoints while in the location.

Being a native Santa Barbaran was an additional challenge for me as a photographer. It was not that there was a shortage of incredible scenery or amazing subjects; I was simply jaded by having familiarized myself throughout the years to what I was now attempting to photograph.

So, I piled both new and old camera equipment into my bag and kept it very handy, hoping to be well equipped and prepared for those times when I felt I could turn the familiar places into images of my hometown, Santa Barbara.